T0148403

CHISELED

Discover Your True Belonging

JULIE ANN SOMERS

iUniverse, Inc.
Bloomington

Chiseled
Discover Your True Belonging

Scripture quotations are based on the New International Version of the Bible, unless otherwise noted.

iUniverse books may be ordered through booksellers or by contacting:

iUniverse
1663 Liberty Drive
Bloomington, IN 47403
www.iuniverse.com
1-800-Authors (1-800-288-4677)

ISBN: 978-1-4502-5673-5 (*pbk*)
ISBN: 978-1-4502-5674-2 (*cloth*)
ISBN: 978-1-4502-5675-9 (*ebk*)

Library of Congress Control Number: 2010913328

Printed in the United States of America

iUniverse rev. date: 2/21/11

CONTENTS

INTRODUCTION

Chisel yourself free from harmful strongholds and discover your true belonging!

With a sense of directness, this book will tell of my life's mishaps, curses and good fortune. And how now, with undaunted devotion, blessings come more frequently as evil subsides. Hopefully as you read, you will be moved in a positive direction that will help you conquer life's constant battles—without spending too much time in the self-help section at your local bookstore like I did! You can find strength through all trials and tribulations no matter where you are. Help is within, and by reaching near to Divinity you will undoubtedly come upon it.

A past coach of mine said: "Most of us are psychological basket cases in one form or another." I believe that in a sensc. In fact, the sufferings I see among others make me realize how wonderful my life really is—while another may look at me and say the same. We all have different stories some worse than the next. Whether it's your health; lack of discipline, motivation, or job; loss of a loved one; struggle with addiction; a difficult relationship—or maybe you have yet to meet your true love and you're spending life alone; we all suffer in one way or another.

Delight in knowing that no matter what your situation, you can learn to pull through any condition—vast or minuscule—by a Divine Power as I have. With strong conviction borne from past and present experiences, I know that God is leading my way. I was led and protected by the Holy Spirit to the point of recognition. Once I became aware of His closeness, I held on to that. And by will, not force, I have continued to carry and fulfill my soul with the most beautifully awaited kinship imaginable. My decision has left me with more confidence, comfort, and joy than I ever dreamed possible.

I am no religious scholar, and my quest is not to try and reel you into some supernatural cult. I am just another fleshly individual making my way, like you.

In this book, I disclose my ongoing endeavors in the hope of helping you have a better understanding of what it takes to fulfill your spiritual being with such life-changing, glorious power.

Allow God to form you from the inside out. Grant Him the right to do the molding while He provides you gear to assist Him.

1

BLOSSOMING BLUES

Childhood Struggles

My ears began to ring from the shock and disbelief as I listened in: "He's dead!" I heard my mother's silent cry as she took the call and soaked in the dreaded news.

I was totally shaken. The phone slipped from my hand and shattered my bedroom mirror. My distress was enhanced from the unintended blast as sadness poured out and alleviation set in.

My mind flashed back to the last time I saw my father with the seductive look on his face as he leered at me with that lustful expression. As I walked though the hallway toward my room, he sat in the living room in only his underwear, kicked back in a recliner, inviting me to join him with physical, but silent overtones. My heart raced like an accelerated time bomb! I continued into my bedroom, bare feet tapping lightly across the hardwood floor, and without much thought, I grabbed a few belongings and crawled out the window. I never saw my daddy again.

It was only a few months following this disturbing incident that my father was pulled from a house fire and taken to the hospital, where he passed away. I was barely a teen at the time of his death.

He had owned a nightclub and was a real estate agent. He had also produced and sold a film about quick change artists and how to detect their motives. On April 17, 1973, he appeared on the Johnny Carson show demonstrating the production. Bob Hope and Karen Valentine were also guest stars on the same show. In 1962, he lost one of his arms on a conveyer belt while working as an inspector in a phosphate mine. I recall my mother frequently assisting him as she strapped and adjusted an artificial limb around his chest before helping clothe him, usually in a suit. He was a handsome man with light hair and blue eyes, but within was a lost frivolous soul.

Today my memories of my father are distant, and thoughts about him are very few. They no longer hold emotion—nothing bitter, nothing sweet—just pretty much forgotten.

Mother's father was an arsenal chemist and was honored by the president of the United States, Harry S. Truman, for his outstanding leadership. He died from spine cancer in 1949. Her mother owned an unemployment operation and worked with medical students as house mom; she eventually passed away in 1981.

Prior to my Grandmother's death, Mom and Dad had eloped and my Nanny was heartsick. Having known my father a few months at the time of their marriage, she was not very fond of him and discouraged their relationship because of his egotistical demeanor. But in a twenty-four year abusive relationship, mother gave birth to seven of his children.

This little black text can't describe my mom's back-bone and the strength she displayed while constantly being lied to and cheated on by my father. She was left alone most of the time to raise five girls and two boys—my twin brother and I being the youngest. Still to this day, she has never let anything come before my siblings and me. Working long shifts at the hospital, my mother clothed and fed us. She instilled morals, manners and love in us to the best of her ability, and ushered us to church almost every Sunday.

This blonde-haired, big blue-eyed, boyish girl with fat cheeks used to love to wear dresses and knee high white boots; my mother couldn't keep a pair of pants on me. After elementary school, I grew out of those frilly skirts and through high school continued with my tomboy ways. I was always very active. Growing up, I was mostly captivated by gymnastics. With all said, mother kept my brothers, sisters and me well rounded in athletics as much as she could afford time-wise and financially. And she let her children choose their specific interests.

We watched her endure humbling pain as she nurtured and loved us all, despite our attitudes of self-defense, insecurities, addictions and overall abusive behavior—we were a very dysfunctional family. But my mother, she never turned her back.

It sounds too coincidental—it's no wonder I felt accountable—first my real dad, then my stepfather: I was awakened from a sound sleep, a hand fondling my privates as I froze in a pretend snooze. It couldn't be the man who finally brightened my mother's world, the one she just married who made her smile like never before, breathing down my back. But it was he who told my mother that while she was working a late night shift he must have been sleepwalking and entered my room thinking I was her.

Do you know how hard it was for me to tell her about that night, about how I tossed and turned until he finally went away? It wasn't the psychological torment from his perverted act that left the blister; it was the thought of my mother brokenhearted once again. True to her nature, she never looked back, and not once did she show self-pity—only concerned love for me. Before you know it, she was divorced with firm will. I admire my mother and have so much respect for her selfless stamina. As for me, I blamed myself.

The trickle effect of these and many other instances in my childhood left me walking around like a rebellious tough girl. If someone so much as looked at me with combative intent I would react like a feeding tiger—of course over-compensating for my fears.

I wondered what it was like to be a normal child in a stable home with parents who actually communicated without strife. I enjoyed watching shows like *Leave It to Beaver, The Brady Bunch* or *Happy Days* because those sitcoms represented the family life I had always wished for. I would dream of dancing on Broadway and acting in award-winning motion pictures. I loved to use my hairbrush as a pretend microphone and sing aloud in the mirror, envisioning myself as I accomplished my dreams with a bright sparkling smile on my face.

I also liked to sit in my room and write poems, which were usually in relation to my wishful fantasies or mental distress. Expressing my emotions on paper helped me get through sad times. I never had trouble finding words to jot down as I put them on that paper-thin cardboard. I believe writing is a God-given talent that helped buffer my innocent mind. A mechanism used by my Divine Designer to sooth my saddened soul.

I played pretend a lot as if things never happened, especially my father's passing. At my age I had a hard time comprehending the meaning of his death. His bizarre innuendo toward me hadn't wiped away the fact that he was still my biological father. So my feelings toward him were not about hate, only confusion. And since I didn't feel outward animosity, I had no idea that I was compiling more grief that would continue to influence me the future.

2

MY FAREWELL

Parting Ways

Living with six siblings who were also affected by their broken and tainted childhoods made me long anticipate my departure from that dark and lonely life. It was tough enough dealing with my personal issues, let alone theirs. At that time, I just wanted to escape it all.

So I left home at the ripe age of 16 determined to find a new life. And I took with me a lot of combative memories. Ashamed of my past, my desire was to start fresh and recreate the person I was. I wanted to make a better impression. I didn't know what kind, but I knew I didn't want to stand for what I thought I stood for, or ever go back to where I had been! Adamant about my sabbatical, nothing would stop me—I counted upon figuring out how as I went.

After my decampment, I became more and more fascinated with dance, mostly aerobic. I enjoyed exercising and following a good diet. Around that time the lifestyle craze first became popular and began to progress. I used to get teased often by friends about my dedication and what I kept in my refrigerator. Still to this day I dance, workout six days a week and practice healthy eating habits. (I will discuss diet and exercise further in a later chapter.)

Although I ran away from my family in hopes for a better life, I continued on a very destructive path. I thought I was OK because I was no longer around all the turmoil of fighting and blaming, but I was still psychologically scarred. I may not have realized it at that time but the subconscious mind doesn't let you forget—maybe having a backup isn't always so good after all!

Bygone days left me with insecurities, low self-esteem and the need to be loved—or perhaps appreciated by others would suffice. In my heart I knew my family cared about me, especially my mother, but I needed to feel accepted by someone outside my family. I was very embarrassed of most of them because of the constant chaos, which many times occurred in public. Of course at that time I didn't take into consideration that their troubled minds were going through the same thing as mine, and probably worse. My brothers in particular have both suffered severely from my father's neglectful ways and sudden death.

My farewell was the beginning of a new chapter in my life, as well as the detachment between me and my family as we all went our separate ways. It was also a period that would dictate to me the responsibilities of a fully matured adult.

3

TRIED AND TRUE

Carrying the Load

At age seventeen, driven and determined to survive on my own, I moved to the small tourist town of Destin, Florida. Eventually, I attended a local community college and worked as a waitress at a popular beachfront restaurant. We got to wear the cutest bikinis with Hawaiian straw skirts and enjoy an atmosphere like paradise with an indoor/outdoor setting and panoramic view of the Gulf of Mexico, alongside snow white sandy beaches. I also worked part-time for a hotel spa called The Healthy Habit.

My thoughts of the past started to lessen like memories at a distance. I was enjoying myself to the fullest; between school, work and pleasure I didn't have time to go down memory lane. But my spent days were sitting right on my sun-kissed shoulder, and although I didn't notice them there, I would bet others did. It's hard to hide beaten down marrow even with a glistening cover. Today, I can spot a tarnished soul miles away—and most likely relate a lot to how the person feels. Just because someone seems to have a picture perfect life doesn't always mean that is the case.

With the little bit of free time I had to socialize while engaged in work and studies, I liked to go to a particular part of the beach where locals gathered. I became friends with what was known as the "in crowd." We would throw Frisbee, play volleyball and enjoy many other beach-related activities. I began hanging out with one guy in particular and my time with him began to increase. He was the one with the cool car that all the girls flocked around. Initially we became good friends, as he always made me feel loved and accepted.

One day he and I were driving down the road and he just blurted out, "You want to get married?" And without much thought, I said, "OK!"

Butterflies didn't really graze my gut as if I had just been proposed to; it was more like Bonnie and Clyde—sex and cigars, just without the violence. He was an adopted military brat, was very intelligent, had traveled the world and attended school in Saudi

Arabia. He loved to fish and hunt, while I was into more active sports. I don't think to this day he has ever seen the inside of a health and fitness club. We had nothing in common yet loved to hang out with each other to fill our empty cups.

The next thing I knew, I was planning a wedding for which his parents would foot the cost. My mother was not very happy about my sudden decision and certainly wasn't going to pay for what she foresaw as an obvious mistake. Isn't it amazing how many times in life you receive the same thing you dished out when you were younger? Yes, my mother got a taste of Grandmother's bitter pie.

Three years into a carefree marriage, I was still waitressing, teaching aerobics and sporadically attending school. I enjoyed working out and going to nightclubs to dance, usually on Wednesday nights—ladies' night—and on the weekends.

My husband ran a bar/restaurant owned by his parents. While working, alcohol consumption became a part of his daily routine. After his shift, he took pleasure in hanging out at pubs where he could drink beer, play pool and throw darts. Our paths were often separated; he was doing what he enjoyed and so was I.

One summer, a girlfriend came to visit for the weekend. We got a wild hare and decided to enter into a "Foxy Lady" contest. (I'm telling my age, huh?) She pleaded with me to enter. I certainly didn't have the courage to do so because I didn't think I would ever have a chance at winning. My friend was very beautiful and had all the confidence in the world. After she saw the other girls who signed up, competitively in her mind she had already stolen the show—and I thought she had too.

Little did I know, dressed in a pastel pink pinstriped men's button-down shirt as a mini-dress, gathered with a big belt to flatter my figure, and high heels shoes, I would place first in that contest. When they called my name I had to pinch myself! Even with the little assurance in me fabricated from vodka and grapefruit juice, I couldn't believe it. As for my long-lost friend, she's probably still pinching herself as well.

WOW! I thought, *how cool is this?* Two hundred and fifty dollars cash prize, a bottle of cheap champagne, suntan lotion and a T-shirt—I felt like I had won the Miss America pageant! That called for a burst of the low-cost bubbles and a 3:00 A.M. breakfast at a local twenty-four-hour diner, on me.

Hardly old enough to drink alcoholic beverages, I had never been exposed to champagne until then. The night ended with my face in the plate of eggs I had ordered, and the next dayspring began with my tongue stuck to the roof of my dehydrated mouth. And the lavatory I once called my powder room became my headquarters most of the day.

Every time I tinkled I noticed an unusual pale green tint in the toxic water. Slow to catch on because of my polluted brain, it dawned on me later that day: I had once heard this was an indication of pregnancy! Standing up in instant shock, eyes as big as golf balls, I dashed to my car and to the drugstore I hurried. I bought a do-it-yourself anytime EPT pregnancy test and scurried home to evaluate my result: two dark lines that appeared to me the size of a freeway no passing zone. *This couldn't be!* Again I bolted out, retracing my footsteps to the drugstore. The second study showed the same score—I was pregnant.

Good grief! I remember thinking; *I haven't mentally ripened since I left my own mother's womb.* I was married to a man I would prefer to call my best friend. And I had concerned thoughts about that sparkling wine frizzling my baby's undeveloped brain as much as it had mine. I asked myself, *where do I go from here?*

So, I slept off my hangover and buckled down, steadfast and determined. I began to research healthy brain development in unborn children, and steamed fish happened to be the claimed hype during that time. I gave up anything and everything harmful to my body, kept a strict workout regime, ate perfectly clean and devoured fishes like a famished grizzly bear.

Soon I was led to a place of comfort where I would gladly prepare myself both mentally and physically. And then I gave birth to a beautiful, healthy, towheaded, green-eyed baby girl with pudgy lips and those same chubby choppers that I once had. We named her Ashley. What a cherished treasure! The first positive outcome from one of my mother's predicted boo-boos.

MY DAUGHTER ASHLEY

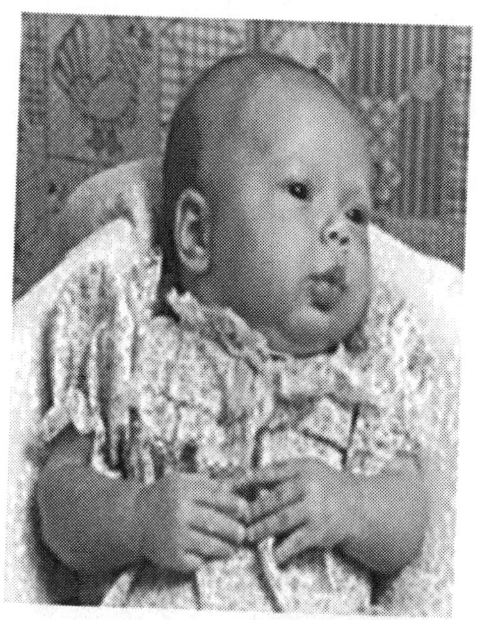

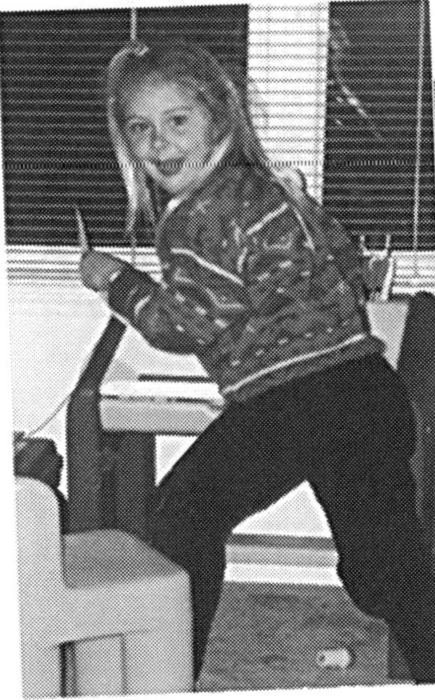

4

COSTLY CUDDLE

Cradling Addiction

Following the birth of our child, serious signs of substance abuse in Ashley's father increased substantially. Although he was constantly encouraged by family and friends to seek help, unfortunately my husband continued to struggle with severe drug and alcohol addiction. This led to our divorce two years later. He was eventually diagnosed with dementia due to his refusal to take notice of his predicament.

Over the course of time, our separation and his condition had a detrimental effect on Ashley, as did the inheritance of her addictive personality from both family trees. By this time, she was an adolescent and I had full custody of her. I wanted to make sure she understood the dangers of her state before it was out of my control, as I had seen how much trouble addiction could cause. So I necessitated inpatient and outpatient treatment on three different occasions, which involved solo and family therapy. She was eventually enrolled into a military school in North Carolina and attended the Scared Straight program in Atlanta, Georgia. It seemed that I had tried everything except a visit to the morgue.

When my daughter blew past eighteen years of age and all of her previous care still wasn't enough, I hoofed it to the local judge's office and pleaded for his help. He informed me of the Marchman Act, a legal provision that provides mandatory care for adults and children who are a threat to society and their own lives. I could file by promising that she had lost the power of self control with respect to substance abuse. That day I followed through with his endorsement. The outcome was successful for the time being, but eventually she was back on the same treacherous path.

Ashley's odd behavior and changing ways had me hanging by a thread. My worrying and *what if* thoughts transpired into months of insomnia. So I began to use my self-taught art skills and created a line of greeting cards. By hand drawing and scanning into Adobe Illustrator, I created a silly, cartoon-like, athletic blonde girl with my daughter's features as a mascot and named her Ashley. She was involved in most sports activities and sent forth messages of only positive affirmations. During our regular family therapy sessions we were taught how to use cognitive reasoning, which teaches how our thoughts control our feelings which in turn control our actions. We learned to think positively by turning a bad thought into a good one. The project was very therapeutic and helped me keep a clear mind and hopeful heart through the course of it all.

Eventually, I had to stop pursuing help for my daughter. I had never seen anyone carry on the way she did. She was so unpredictable that I had to turn my back on her—with nothing but love in my bleeding heart. We are very close. She couldn't believe that I would actually let her hit rock bottom because prior to this torturous time I never had the guts to do it. But after years of professional advice, I knew that was what it was going to take.

From that point on, Ashley began to face and accept her problem. Unlike her father, she is now fully educated about drug abuse and addiction. Well aware of her weaknesses, she resides in South Florida where she attends school and is majoring in technical design and drafting.

Ashley has a background in gymnastics, cheerleading and keyboard, but her real love is tennis. She also enjoys reading, has a passion for animals and favors cats. She is very well liked, especially by children. Her potential comes through like a beam of light when she is not under the control of substances. She will offer so much to society as she continues her revival.

I didn't realize it at the time, but the more I focused on Ashley and helped aid in her childhood difficulties the less I thought about my troubles. My motherly instinct definitely kicked in when it was needed. Was that God's way of beginning maturity for me? Was it a configuration of the rest of my life depicted by my invisible Comforter? I believe it was.

EXAMPLES OF MY GREETING CARDS

No matter what the season,
for any reason...

Inside: You can count on me!

5

BUNCHES AND BABYLOVE

Making It Last (Relationships)

"I do!"

Ten years into a happy-go-lucky relationship the question was popped. It was a cold and rainy day with a festive-like ambiance and the sound of Christmastime. We toured Central Park in New York City in a carriage pulled by a white horse and Frenchman. Kneeling before me was the most beautiful creature and man of my dreams. I felt the sweep of a masculine hand as he reached in his shirt pocket for the special gemstone. With orderly focus and a teary-eyed, gorgeous smile, "Will you marry me?"

I was tucked away in a sheep's wool blanket, mucky from the climatic conditions, when the ring of wedded bliss took my frosty breath away. I gladly agreed to his proposal.

Yes, ten years had passed before this happy day. We nestled under the same roof during that time, of course accompanied by my daughter. The young father figure and go-getter himself, my soon-to-be husband, John Paul, by that time had built our dream house resting on ambition and faith. At the time he worked as vice president of a medical rehabilitation company, and I worked in outside sales for a geotechnical environmental firm. As if we had already tied the knot, we were settled in a very nice neighborhood in Dunwoody, Georgia, amidst a good school and a church where my daughter was involved in many youth activities.

As easygoing as was our bond, we still struggled with the ups and downs of everyday life. Raising a child from a divorced family and dealing with personal issues summoned us to the test on many occasions, but our fondness for one another kept us together through it all. John Paul's well-founded determination left him stable on very fickle and wobbly grounds. Between playing the role of stepfather at a tender age and dealing with both my and Ashley's uncertainties, he is without a doubt a man of integrity and complete devotion—and I am awfully grateful.

Friends and family scrutinized the length of time we had been together in relation to the tie that binds. But their words flowed in one ear and out the other as we overlooked the immoral aspect of our lives. I am not suggesting living together or sex before marriage, but I do recommend not rushing into a commitment. Many race to walk down the aisle out of desperation and end up in divorce.

If you are waiting for Mr. or Mrs. Right, never show eagerness to settle down with someone as it only discounts self-sufficiency. And it may scare them silly and send them on their merry way. Instead find peace with yourself, and as you are pleased as punch, they will most likely start sniffing your flavors!

During the many years my husband and I were together prior to marriage, I never gave a hint of wedding bells. In fact, when the topic cropped up after someone else's mention, I would tease him and say, "If you ever ask me to marry you, you had better be on a white horse dressed as a knight in shining armor!" That is how the stallion came in the dreamy scene on our engagement day. John Paul wasn't actually on that bronco, but that was good enough for me.

When I think about the gobs of women on this planet, the sensation overwhelms me that this charming young man chose to spend the rest of his life with me. I wish for everyone such connection and dream come true. I believe that somewhere out there is a Romeo for every woman.

Yet many who are blessed to find a mate tend to take their favored situation for granted. Instead of seeing it as an honor, they often change, domineering their spouses or letting their appearances and motivation levels dwindle. It's as if they had falsely concocted themselves until their partners were hooked.

With marriage, it is common for lovemaking to gradually lessen as time goes by. But once united as husband and wife, the candy making shouldn't stop there! You should never let adoration go stale. In fact, let your gratefulness show with a delightful attitude and simple little love touches that don't cost a coin. Kiss, mate and laugh. Keep yourself up and the love alive! By the way, Bunches and Babylove (he and I) are the goofy names we dubbed one another years ago. Silly things like that mean a lot in a relationship, believe it or not!

> **1 Corinthians 7:2-3** – *"But since there is so much immorality, each man should have his own wife, and each woman her own husband. The husband should fulfill his marital duty to his wife, and likewise the wife to her husband."*

John Paul and I are approaching twenty years together and have more fun now than ever. Having met at a party, we knew nothing about one another at first, and of course we didn't agree about every subject matter. So naturally it has taken effort from both of us to get to this point. Many couples give up in a relationship before ever getting to the best part. It is when differences have been ironed out with love and understanding that the battle is overcome. That alone will make a coupling tough to replace.

Relationships are hard-won. Everyone is different and anytime you put two people together they are going to clash at some point. Whether it is best friends, sisters, mother and daughter, or husband and wife, controversy will arise. Know how to deal with your differences by understanding that you don't think alike because you aren't alike, so you have to learn to compromise.

Always remember, with petty feuds it's OK to say you're sorry even if it's not your fault. Do what you can to keep your jungle green for the sake of both of you. And you can't sweat little habits that bug you about the other. Instead, without trying to change your mate, gracefully play off both demeanors with self composure—and eventually it will make for a gratifying love concoction.

Compliment your soul mate. I was talking to a friend of mine over the phone about a short spat I had just had with my husband. She said to me, "You shouldn't tell him how good-looking he is all the time." (I do this quite often, yet he always gives me warm fuzzy praises too. And not just about the way we look on the outside, which continues to fade over time, but also about the nature of one another's character.) Well, that was pretty much the only thing that I have ever heard flow from her mouth that I didn't agree with.

Everyone wants to feel good about him or herself—and I can't think of a more perfect person to have spread the icing than your significant other. After all, attraction in one way or another is what brought you together in the first place. Therefore, doesn't it make good sense to continue with the flattery since you plan to spend the rest of your lives together? If you don't applaud your lover, then you are putting an unnecessary damper on your environment and your relationship. This can be the reason why eyes begin to wander and one may fly from the cuckoo's nest. No one wants to live in a gloomy world.

Your life's picture is how you paint it when faced with rises and falls. So make your future a brighter place together, as one.

Genesis 2:24 – *"For this reason a man will leave his father and mother and be united to his wife, and they will become one flesh."*

The Song of Songs 1:15-16 –

He: *"How beautiful you are, my darling! Oh, how beautiful! Your eyes are doves."*

She: *"How handsome you are, my lover! Oh, how charming! And our bed is verdant."*

6

DELIVERANCE

Rescued by My Savior

How did I make it to this point? I was living a life noteworthy of a fairytale, yet my heart and soul were ransacked with bleeding wounds.

The following mishaps are now closed chapters in my life, yet they comprise a crucial part of this book. By God's grace, they have become loopholes that have led me out of the darkness and into the light.

> **Philippians 3:13-14** – "*Brothers, I do not consider myself yet to have taken hold of it. But one thing I do: Forgetting what is behind and straining toward what is ahead, I press on toward the goal to win the prize for which God has called me heavenward in Christ Jesus.*"

I will briefly describe these diverse events in the order in which they occurred.

One of the incidents that began my two-year nightmare was botched dentistry on my nearly perfect, natural pearly whites. But it is a topic I refuse to rehash in detail as it brings about so many bad memories. I disallow it to take away from another minute of my valuable journey.

I suddenly became like a newborn klutz—with never-ending blemishes from constant cuts and bangs. My skin became dry and splotchy, my hair brittle, and the self-esteem and confidence that I had finally built up went down the tube as fast as a liquid drain cleaner. At times I was unable to control my bowels, I had daily hot flashes and night sweats, and my orgasms were the pits! I felt helpless and tapped out as the "disasters" continued to prevail. My husband didn't know who I was anymore, nor did I.

At the time, I was unaware of my depleted hormone levels, although my monthlies had come to a halt. A while later I was told by my gynecologist that I was post menopausal and would never have another period again—something I didn't want to hear in my thirties.

My brain was so scrambled from the chemical deficiency that it took me an hour to pay two bills. With the inability to carry on an intelligent conversation, I came across as ignorant—and knew it. I only heard a fraction of what people would say to me from such a short attention span. The torment carried on for a good year and a half. I had never felt so bad about myself and my lack of self-control, but I continued to pray, without much clarity of thought.

One sunny day my husband and I took a stroll in a nearby cottage beach town for a fun-filled day. Pretending to "be happy" and "feel good" so I didn't disappoint him any more than I already had, I stopped for a potty break to find the most astonishing discovery: bright red blood—and a lot of it. What a beautiful sight! Same doctor, second test showed I was not post menopausal. So back on the roller coaster I went.

While living in Los Angeles, I visited with a hormone therapy specialist in Santa Monica. She got me back on a stable thoroughfare using bio-identical (plant-derived) hormone creams. The treatment helped balance out my—come to find—exercise-induced exhausted supply.

My future began to look somewhat brighter, until a long-awaited minor procedure rolled around. I had the raised lesion removed on a twenty-year-old C-section scar hidden very low below my panty line.

Along with it I opted for a little skin tightening on my cheeks—what the surgeon described as "a piece of cake" that would leave small incisions in front of either ear which would blend in with my natural creases.

After the operation, I awakened to find my entire head wrapped in bandages and a very sore black-and-blue stomach. The doctor had decided to liposuction my well-toned lower abs right above the scar to "smooth it out." The results left me with discoloration and lumps on my once attractive belly, cuts completely around my ears, and chopped earlobes sewn directly to my face! *What have I done? My good-looking stomach now distorted and the natural curvature in my lobes, gone!* This flop added massive bulk to my rotten apple cart.

But it wasn't over yet. A few months into an unsatisfactory recovery from the surgeries, I went to the dentist complaining of a toothache. While I was enduring that ongoing disaster, she informed me I needed a root canal. Later that week she began the procedure as it consisted of multiple visits. Upon my return home from my first appointment, I looked in the mirror and noticed one side of my face had fallen. Usually healthy, wholesome and fit, I now resembled someone who had a major stroke! My left eye wouldn't shut, I couldn't smile or pucker my lips, and I drooled all over myself.

After an immediate trip to a local neurologist, I was informed I had Bell's palsy. This condition is triggered from extreme stress but stems from a virus that supposedly lives dormant in ninety percent of the U.S. population—herpes simplex. It is also associated with shingles, chicken pox and fever blisters. Although this sudden disorder can be ongoing, the bug usually settles and generally goes away within weeks to a few months. But due to my stress load, my face stayed paralyzed for about a year.

If you know anyone with this condition, or unfortunately experience it yourself, be sure to see a doctor who specializes in Bell's palsy. I met with a speech pathologist who advised me to exercise my face daily. This resulted in another condition called synkinesis, which causes involuntary muscle movement. It is very difficult to treat. Eventually, John Paul flew me to Washington, D.C., to the Bell's Palsy Research Foundation for further evaluation and much-needed advice, which led to almost one hundred percent recovery.

As if every other prior setback wasn't enough, during a rigorous bike ride to the gym one Sunday afternoon,

John Paul and I took an alternate route home before our planned sushi dinner that evening. The shout of my husband's voice as he screamed my name caused me to quickly turn my handlebars. This saved me from being crushed under a trailer carrying a boat being pulled by a car. Instead, I was hit in the head, sideswiped by the watercraft and thrown off my bicycle onto the concrete in front of oncoming traffic. Thankfully the forging cars had enough time to come to a screeching stop.

After being supported by braces and male medics while transported to the hospital, I was discharged with a few staples in the back of my noggin and minor road burns. Not one sprain or broken bone! That called for a hat over my blood-drenched hair and a taste of those longed-for Japanese rolls. I was so grateful to be alive, thanks to God!

Just one week later, on an airplane flight, I couldn't believe my ears. Some men were laughing and joking about the smoke as it filled the cabin of the MD-88 ten minutes into the air. Our captain announced we had lost all electrical power and then warned us that he had to turn the plane around. I thought my life was over! My taut forehead rested on John Paul's shoulder as I prayed out loud for our safety. The fifteen minutes it took to land and exit the air jet seemed like hours, but everyone made it off unharmed.

That was it! I couldn't take any more close calls. I knew my affairs were miniscule compared to others, but the trials were coming way too often and without ceasing. Upon my return home, I had never felt so weak and tired. I fell to my knees in a wailing plea, *"God, help remove this black cloud that hovers above me. I need You so badly, Father, please come into my life."*

In that breath, weight lifted from me. Suddenly, I felt protected and unafraid. I have always prayed, but I have never felt such instant relief as I did at that remarkable moment. Nothing will ever convince me that I was not lifted from despair by my All-Powerful Maker, Father God. Since that day, good has triumphed evil, and the misadventures have gradually died away.

It's most likely I will never know why I was put to the test around the clock for two solid years. Perhaps my lack of loyalty with respect to our Heavenly Father left me unshielded. I really can't say for sure. But now I carry on, constantly crushing self-destructive obstacles. As my faith sweetly evolves, adversities whittle away. And until I am sculpted and molded pleasingly in the eyes of God, I will continue carefully cutting and cleaving, with prayer, trust and love by acts of kindness.

The thought of those gentlemen laughing agitated me on the plane that day because I was so terrified, but I know now what total trust means when I think back and hear the laughter of those faithful followers sitting next to me. In fact, their certainty probably brought us home safely. I have a strong desire for such unwavering faith, which time and diligence shall bring.

> **James 4:7** – *"Submit yourselves, then, to God. Resist the devil, and he will flee from you."*

7

HOPEFUL HEARTS

Keeping the Faith

During my prolonged liberation, John Paul's family was facing their own dilemmas. My husband has one brother and two sisters. His youngest sister, Lesley, suffered brain damage from a car wreck in the bustling streets of Atlanta, Georgia. She was working in outside sales at the time of her accident. Oddly enough, she had just recovered from a coma resulting from another head-on collision while plugging away for the same corporation. The company had just voted her "top performer" and awarded Lesley a car for her superlative sales. In a moment I will share a special story about Lesley's outcome.

On November 22, 1992, John Paul's father died from gallbladder cancer. My guess would be that Lesley's condition was a contributing factor to his speedy downfall. Mr. Somers had been an influential corporate patent attorney and was employed by AT&T for over thirty years. After his death, he was recognized for successfully patenting cutting-edge fiber optics technologies, which are widely used today. His family proudly accepted that award on his behalf.

Between her husband's death and daughter's ill-fortune, John Paul's mother had taken a beating. And from that point to this day, John's willingness to fully aid in his mother's care has reassured me of his genuine character. His mother resided next to us for several years and we spent much of our time together. From dining to travels to sunset walks on the beach, we've had a lot of fun times worth storing in the memory as she is a joy to be around. He and his mother are very close. He describes her as "the best mother in the world," and she labels him as her special gift since he was her last-born and was surprisingly unexpected.

In 2006, Ms. Somers was diagnosed with Parkinson's disease. At that time she and her children decided it would be best for her to live with her daughter and grandchildren, which she did. For several years she kept herself busy being involved in their activities, and also helping around the house.

As signs of her illness have rapidly increased, she now resides with John Paul and me as we provide her the best possible care, which she deserves.

Her daughter Lesley was incapacitated following the accident and was being cared for at The Jimmy Simpson Foundation (TJSF) in Rocksprings, Georgia, close to the Tennessee line. Specializing in traumatic brain injuries, TJSF is a Christian-oriented facility where twenty-four-hour care is provided. During our stop-overs I always noticed how clean the house was throughout—especially around the baseboards where you couldn't find one speck of dust bunnies! Lesley was always freshly showered upon our arrivals, even though many times our visits were unexpected. She couldn't have stayed at a better place considering her devastating condition.

By 2008, despite having been in a vegetative state for fifteen years, Lesley still wasn't giving up. Her health was maintained through the nourishment of an IV as her cognitive mode gradually diminished. It had gotten to the point where she didn't know who her family was during our grievous visitations with her. It was very disheartening to us knowing she had suffered that long. And the only thing we knew that was left to do was pray for a miracle.

Back in our home state, John Paul and I had friends over one evening. As we were sitting and babbling, his sister Lesley was brought up. John Paul explained what had happened to her and how he couldn't understand why she wouldn't just wake up or let go.

Our friend Gary said, it could be that God is prompting her to hang on until she establishes her eternal security with Him—maybe she is waiting to exchange seeds." He continued, "It's possible she never had the opportunity to ask God for forgiveness and she wants to swap her corruptible seed for her incorruptible one." At the time we were not familiar with that part of scripture so our curiosity had us listening intently as he explained.

> **1 Peter 1:23** – *"For you have been born again, not of perishable seed, but of imperishable, through the living and enduring word of God."*

Although Lesley could not speak and we were not always sure about her ability to mentally comprehend, Gary reminded us that the human spirit is on another level than the mind and body. He encouraged us to go visit and pray with her to make this request to God.

Without question, the next morning John Paul had the car packed and we were headed to the Tennessee border.

The day was sunny and beautiful so we asked the nurses if we could roll Lesley and her wheelchair out to the gazebo behind the dwelling, which we did. The setting was very peaceful and the time felt right, yet we were feeling a bit apprehensive about what to say. So John Paul and I decided to call Gary from my cell phone and ask him to pray for Lesley while on speakerphone. And he did, gladly so. John Paul was on one side of Lesley and I was on the other as we cradled her in prayer. During the midst of our prayerful moment, we watched as a brimming teardrop rolled down Lesley's face. Surprised by the dewy trace, we braced her as he ended the blessing.

Within a few months, on Thanksgiving Day—and the same date of John Paul's father's death—we received a call. Dear Lesley had passed away.

In many cases an individual will go to great extent to pleasantly take his or her journey alone before finally realizing: he can't. And that is usually when he turns to God for a helping hand. Attempting your lifelong hike solo doesn't make you wrong. Most of us don't understand. Our enemy does everything possible to keep us blinded from the truth as long as he can.

Don't wait to be unshackled. Free yourself of the sorrows from our enemy's wicked ways. Connect with God now and live a peaceful life with Him guarded from harm. And make certain you have accepted God's way to your eternal home in the great unknown.

LESLEY CAROL SOMERS
AUGUST 27, 1965 - NOVEMBER 22, 2007

THE SOMERS FAMILY

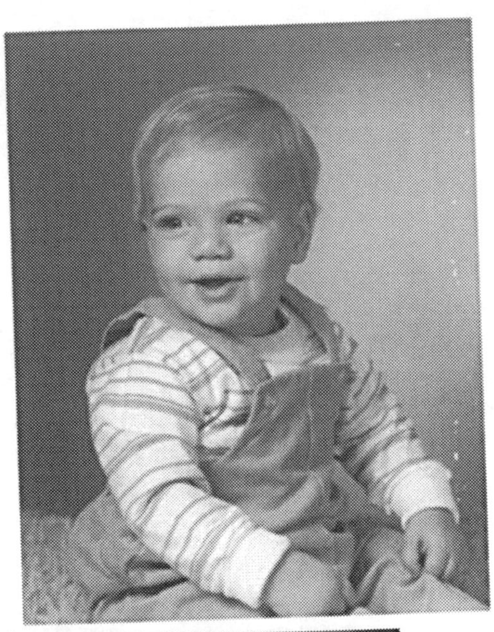

JOHN PAUL SOMERS

8
FREEDOM
Easily Unshackled

Can't dance, sing, drink or be merry. It's no wonder people are afraid to seek God! They are under the impression they have to give up everything fun in their earthly lives to have a healthy relationship with their Lord and Savior. Society has us believing that if you do anything fun you are going to hell.

What many fail to realize is the king of the inferno is the force behind such lies, and that same coward who rules this planet has brainwashed humanity to mental disarray. Each of us dealing with different dilemmas, one more awkward than the next, moving in every direction trying to find answers. Imagine an army of ants swarming among their self-made dune: although they truly have a mission, it appears as if they are lost and going around in circles. That's what the evil one wants us to do. He wants us to harbor sin and feel confused so hope is lost, so that we are left in the dark with no confidence or self-esteem. He yearns to steal your joy, your relationships, your health, even your life—and he will if you let him.

The devil has full control of your existence, unless you seek God's love and guidance by simply and sincerely asking Him to save you.

Know that He is more powerful than all—even that evil little pest and his army can't pull the wool over Almighty God! All you have to do is put your total trust in Him. This means you have to open up with courage, faith and the will to believe the unknown and unseen. Know in your heart you are healed by Jesus' stripes; know that you will have healthy relationships and a steady job. You have to believe the miraculous happenings of God's mysterious workings just like the ones written in the earliest books of the Bible. And eventually, blessings will begin to shower on your troubled world. God's heart aches with the woe of your sorrow. He wants nothing more than to see you happy while in His love. And if you genuinely come unto Him so that you may have life, He will gladly give it to you.

I never knew what true happiness was until I offered Him the driver's seat. And since then I have felt chauffeured around as if in a brand-new Bentley. Sure, we've hit road bumps and approached dead-end streets, but only when I have tried to take over and become backseat driver. As long as you trust Him as your cabby to drive and guide you, you will go on the most extraordinary ride of your life!

Wouldn't you rather chance it than not? After all, what do you have to lose? What do you already have that you wouldn't trade for good health, happiness, love and riches? It's your journey; the choices you make determine its quality. It's up to you. God is a loving God and a forgiving God. He will do so much for you and continue to bless you as you grow closer and closer to His kingdom.

There are so many myths about Christianity. And philosophers are still trying to find answers to God's well-kept secrets; many stumpers continue to be perplexing. Often there seems to be no justice; sometimes the wicked prosper and the righteous suffer.

Again, I am no historian or biblical expert. But I do know that from experience I have witnessed good angels and fallen angels, curses and freedom in a way that has moved my soul to an unbending belief that will never be stripped away from me.

This understanding has left me confident, happy and hopeful, knowing I am loved while surrounded by divine defenders, my guardian angels.

No one will ever know the absolute truth until we receive full revelation from God regardless of how much research is involved. It may be rightly guessed but unrevealed until the end. Personally, I believe we will receive a reply to all of our unanswered questions from our Father God come judgment day. So while left speculating, why not let Him present to you your future as He demonstrates each day—a life full of hope and gladness? A good rapport with God will bring you more peace and understanding than you will find from anything, anyone, anywhere in this universe. Go for it and do not be afraid.

As humans we have to search deep within ourselves while fighting off those beastly demons that try and hinder us from seeing that if we truly believe in our hearts and souls that Jesus died on the cross for our sins, we will be saved. I don't expect everyone to believe what I'm convinced of, and I never judge those who don't, as that is not my right. But I know from my personal experience that as I pray without doubt and build on my faith, my life gets better and better. And the more joyful I am, the more I want to pray and worship His name. And the more I worship His name, the more doors He opens for me. He's present—as He keeps showing me—right by my side at all times. What a powerful consciousness!

> **Psalm 16:8** – "*I have set the Lord always before me. Because He is at my right hand, I will not be shaken.*"

When those little baneful bugs realize you aren't afraid anymore they don't come around as often, but they never completely go away. They will hammer you when least expected, especially when they know you are vulnerable. Often they attack when you're tired or stressing over a certain situation, and they always try to oppose those seeking spiritual conversion. But as long as you stand firm and bind the vicious villains from your life by profuse prayer in Jesus' name, He will carry you through. If you truly believe He is protecting you, you will be astounded as affirmation overflows you.

> **Psalm 3:6** – "*I will not fear the tens of thousands drawn up against me on every side.*"

Pray always, not only in time of need or just for yourself. Brace your family, friends, our nation and strangers too. So many people need your prayers. You will be amazed how you can make a difference in others' lives by pleading with God while shining His light! And when you pray, plead in the Holy Ghost, then sit and listen while you meditate. Don't just let words roll off your tongue without reflecting. Also, always thank Him for the many blessings that begin to flow through your life. He loves to be praised! And never watch for something bad to befall you; always expect good things to come.

When you make a decision to let God rule your roost, it doesn't mean your life stops there. He doesn't condemn you or judge you. Just as He has continued to chisel me throughout my life, He will constantly cleanse and spiritually mold you little by little. And while doing so you both reap the benefits as you walk in His way. He will do things that will then make you realize what those who are already on that pathway were talking about that previously you never understood and they couldn't explain.

As your life unfolds spiritually, He will make known to you many little things you've been trying to figure out for so long. And you will grow more Heaven-ward the more fascinated you become. He wants you to ask for His guidance. He loves to see your dimples sink in and your smile light up when you feel His presence. Let me assure you that everything from God is of love and light. And to acquire that love all you have to do is ask, believe and trust in Him. How liberating!

Expect those evil gnats to start swarming when they realize your chosen favor. They will do everything possible to turn you away from your holy focus. If you are living your life constantly trying to figure out how to please your Father, yet feeling like you're not good enough, that is worry and worry is not from God. You were forgiven the day you asked for His forgiveness and for Him to come into your life. Now all you have to do is ask Him to make your path straight while you are led by the Holy Spirit. As you walk joyfully in grace with the Lord, He will not condemn you but will protect you when you are bombarded.

Now, put all of your troubles (guilt, fear, blame, resentment, etc.) in a padlocked chest and leave it with your Father. Let Him be responsible, not you.

> **John 3:16-18** – "*For God so loved the world that He gave His one and only Son, that whoever believes in Him shall not perish but have eternal life. For God did not send His Son into the world to condemn the world, but to save the world through Him. Whoever believes in Him is not condemned, but whoever does not believe stands condemned already because he has not believed in the name of God's one and only Son.*"

Some may wonder what made me choose to believe that Jesus suffered on that cross for our salvation. And I will tell you, it wasn't like I made a mental decision; it was a Spirit within that ultimately placed that certitude upon me. But, had I not been enlightened, and was forced to decide something to regard as true, my thoughts would have swayed toward deeming this powerful miracle valid. Why? Because I have yet to hear of another way to escape condemnation, and where there is hope I will go.

9

SACRED WORDS

The Key to Happiness

In 2001, something came over me; I began speculating my beliefs and disbeliefs. At the time I realized that everything I deemed as true was what other common people just like me—Julie as an individual—convinced me of. So I made a decision to read the Bible from beginning to end. I wanted to find out what was in that book instead of listening to what everyone told me I should believe. And I asked myself, *Will I believe it?*

I am no avid reader by any means, but I decided to read the Holy Bible while working out on my Stairmaster at home, for one hour almost every day. I began in the Old Testament. Although I only understood a fraction of what was written, I had made a promise to myself that I would read word for word no matter what, so I carried forward with my commitment.

Several weeks into my obligation one horrific day took place: September 11th. I remember feeling like the world was coming to an end. For most of us that was a very eerie and sad day. How do you explain the inexplicable?

After the tragedies, my inner self told me to skip the rest of the Old Testament and begin again in the New Testament. So I did. While admittedly I did not complete reading all the Hebrew Scriptures (Old Testament), I felt proud and accomplished when I completed my task. And although I read that Book of books, I had yet to get the picture as it was very hard for me to make sense of it all.

Now and then I would open and read wherever my peepers landed in hopes of a better understanding. Surprisingly, so many times I would come to a place I could follow that talked about what was troubling me at that time. You will be amazed at the hint of glorious wonders God startles you with right in the nick of time when you read Scripture and seek His companionship.

> **1 Peter 5:6-7** – *"Humble yourselves, therefore, under God's mighty hand, that He may lift you up in due time. Cast all your anxiety on Him because He cares for you."*

I finally realized that this manual (the Holy Bible) is a directory—a very sacred and authoritative guidebook—that is the key to your happiness if you make it part of your everyday life by reading it as often as you can. I'm convinced it will pave the way to your eternal being. And can you imagine the ancient historical knowledge you garner? After all, the entire book is filled with non-contradictory testimonies.

If you are having a hard time believing His Word and the stories written by His disciples but are curious, be willing to give it a whirl. Don't rack your brain trying to figure it all out because you never will. Trust in God's safekeeping just like a child depends on his mother for nurturing.

> **Hebrews 4:12** – *"For the word of God is living and active. Sharper than any double-edged sword, it penetrates even to dividing soul and spirit, joints and marrow; it judges the thoughts and attitudes of the heart."*

Read scripture and pray endlessly. God is your forever sidekick; you can talk to Him no matter where you are. I have a tendency to blabber to Him out loud, in public. Not too loud though—no one can hear me except myself and Him, although they may see my lips move. :o) You don't have to go to that extent of course, but when He sees that you are sincerely seeking Him, He will latch onto you. And when He does, you will know it.

1 John 3:24 – *"The one who keeps God's commands live in Him, and He in them. And this is how we know that He lives in us. We know it by the spirit He gave us."*

Then, you should shield yourself with His whole armor that you may withstand the slyness of evil. That bulletproof protective covering is made of:

The Belt of Truth – *helps you know the truth about God (Deuteronomy 4:39; Psalm 23:1; 18:1-3).*

The Breastplate of Righteousness – *allows Jesus to live in you (Psalm 100:3; Romans 3:23-24; 6:23; Galatians 2:20-21; 3:8-10).*

Sandals of Peace – *bring inner peace and readiness (Romans 5:1; Ephesians 2:14; John 14:27; 16:33; 20:21).*

The Shield of Faith – *helps you to live by faith (Romans 4:18-21; Hebrews 11:1; 1 Peter 1:6-7).*

The Helmet of Salvation – *comes from salvation through Christ today and forever (Ephesians 6:13-17).*

The Sword of the Spirit – *which is God's Word, counters spiritual deception and accusations (Hebrews 4:12; Matthew 4:1-11; Psalm 119:110-112).*

And upon His Son's return you will possess both God's Word and promise—an eternal life in Heaven, a peaceful wonderland beyond imagination.

Why would anyone want to pass that up?

10

SPOKEN

Words Are Powerful

At birth you are appointed channels that are connected to God the Father, the Son and the Holy Spirit, who are one (the Trinity). It is up to you to eventually activate those links of Divinity though the Holy Spirit. Such activation couldn't be easier—or more delightfully relieving for the weary soul. He is ready for that joining whenever you are and loves you no matter what.

He already knows your heart, so lift Him up in all sincerity as you humble yourself though prayer and petition. This lets Him know you are willing to accept the fact that there is no other way to freedom except through His Son Jesus' lovely vine. Jesus said to His disciples at the last supper, "*I am the vine; you are the branches. If a man remains in Me and I in him, he will bear much fruit; apart from Me you can do nothing*" **(John 15:5).**

Once attached to this sacred plant, it is up to you to keep your offshoots fruitful. One very good way to start is by speaking positive affirmations about your life no matter what you are dealing with.

> **Psalm 103:1-8** of David says:
>
> "Praise the Lord, O my soul; all my inmost being, praise His holy name. Praise the Lord, O my soul, and forget not all His benefits— who forgives all your sins and heals all your diseases, who redeems your life from the pit and crowns you with love and compassion, who satisfies your desires with good things so that your youth is renewed like the eagle's. The Lord works righteous and justice for all the oppressed. He made known His ways to Moses, His deeds to the people of Israel: The Lord is compassionate and gracious, slow to anger, abounding in love."

This is what the vine is made of: love not hate, health not sickness, peace not war. And when you shout praise to His name, those promises you will get. When you are sick, don't claim it. Thank God for healing all your ailments. When feeling snappy, then rather smile. Don't let Satan have his way. Because when you give way to the negative, your branch becomes barren and falls from the tree, and you grow helpless. If this does happen, begin again knowing your loving God understands.

It's not easy, but you can teach yourself how to stay positive with practice. Use cognitive reasoning. If you speak sickness, there is a greater chance you will have it; talk poverty, and it will be. But if you utter worth, wellness and better days ahead, it's likely you will be gifted with these sacred treasures.

Just remember, real gifts come from faithfulness whether or not all of our prayers, hopes and expectations are answered exactly the way would like them to be.

Voice God's love with a trusting heart as you show your loyalty to Him. And when He sees your assuredness, His mercy will follow. You can go to church on Sundays and do all good works to try and earn your rewards for Heaven and a better earthly life. But without devout faith, you're choking your hope. So, let the words of your breath be graciously heard straight from your believing heart.

11

SHINE

Slather the World with Love

As we drift along on this big blue marble, devoting never-ending steadfast love to others, we are reflecting the glory of God. His two greatest commandments are to love our God and our neighbor. Let's face it: in today's world, with such prevailing hatred, loving everyone seems almost impossible. But upholding these commandments is easier than you think. Forgiveness and letting go of resentment will allow you to express genuine affection to others. And as described in the last chapter, the more positive we are—especially toward our neighbors—the more magnificent our lives will be because we are gratifying our Heavenly Father who in return will fulfill our needs.

God doesn't rank us on how much we know about sacred writings or how often we attend church. Our fruitfulness to Him is how much love is in our hearts. When God made known His actuality to me, all I knew of the Bible and theology was Adam, Eve and the apple tree, nothing of the seven angels talked about in the book of Revelation. It is when I discovered His actual existence that I thirsted for a better understanding. Now, I commit the good news to mind. And like a child, I walk in trust while traveling through the darkness. I shine His light on others with a glimmer of hope that they may see this narrow pathway that leads to Him. You see, He uses us to help others find that alleyway, and from there He does the teaching and blessing. And throughout life He will intermittently use us as a teacher's tool.

Once you are found, stay the course and don't give up because other roads are hazardous and will lead to wreckage. Should you find yourself shambled in despair, just keep dazzling your shimmering light. God sees your encounter; He's got your back! Unfortunately, there is no getting around Satan throwing stones, but by pleasantly trusting you can control the receiver.

We are in this life for a purpose and God's ulterior motive for us is not material things, wealth or popularity—as without Him they are but nothingness. The whole idea behind His objective is to use us as guiding lights to show others the way to eternal life, so they may live victoriously with Him as originally planned.

The only thing I regret about alighting upon this angelic avenue is that I didn't find it sooner. Some wait until fate is looming in the distance and never experience the optimal odyssey while living this existence. Don't wait—get it while you can. And enjoy it! Now I highly value and get a charge out of my life because I know I can't control it. I can dictate my thoughts and actions, but I can't arbitrate a precise future. So all I have to do is trust and take pleasure in blessings as I slather the world with love and affection, and by doing so I automatically shine. How hard is that? SHINE, SHINE, SHINE!

> **Matthew 28:18-20** – *"Then Jesus came to them and said, 'All authority in heaven and on earth has been given to Me. Therefore go and make disciples of all nations, baptizing them in the name of the Father, and of the Son and of the Holy Spirit, and teaching them to obey everything I have commanded you. And surely I am with you always, to the very end of age.'"*

12

JUDGE NOT!

Focus on What Matters

The key element to spiritual growth is reinforcement of our very own superstructure. The goal is to not only appear untainted from the outside but to allow purification to seep all the way through our hearts and souls to our bones. We must build enough strength within to overpower adversity by changing the way we think, feel and act.

She's fat. He has no morals. Look at the acne on that person's face! Have you often found yourself thinking such critical thoughts? Most commonality does. Regardless of what we see in someone, our belittling remarks—spoken or voiceless—are unwarranted. If something is obvious about someone and he or she can help it, either they don't know about it, they couldn't care less, or they may have an underlying issue holding them back. And as far as physical flaws, remember we are all configurations of God; none of us get to choose the way we look when we are born.

The same goes for our intellect. If God gave each of us equal smarts—which certainly isn't the case—our mental capacity or expertise would still vary from person to person because none of our tutelages are the same. Childhood rearing, guardianship and schooling are all different with each individual. Stupidity to me is wasting time comparing IQ's or looks when we can use that energy learning something new. Even Einstein had room for improvement. Instead of passing judgment, have compassion for others, as they may already be unhappy with their intelligence level, personal appearance or personality.

If you bad-mouth someone because that individual's principles or actions are not up to your standard, that is a battle within yourself. Your judgment of him or her automatically makes you wrong because you find fault with that person. We are all trapped in sin at some point in our lives. Jesus is perfect, yet He never judged the prostitute. No one was excluded when He came to die for the sins of mankind.

> **Matthew 21:31** – "*Which of the two did what his father wanted?*" "The first," they answered. Jesus said to them, "*I tell you the truth, the tax collectors*

> *and the prostitutes are entering the Kingdom of God ahead of you."*

The irony of it is that judging is unjustified. No two people are just alike; we are all living souls with different characteristics. One person's impression of someone is most likely different than the next individual's. Therefore, it is senseless to think that your vote is correct.

> **Matthew 7:3** asks, "*Why do you look at the speck of sawdust in your brother's eye and pay no attention to the plank in your own eye?*"

That assertion makes a lot of sense. When we are quick to judge our neighbors, we are usually sending out insecurity signals about ourselves. A sour opinion of someone reveals the self-doubt or swaggering tail of the one scrutinizing. And if you are swaying that behind, remember, an egotistical personality will take away from your character whether you are a head turning stunner or rolling in the riches.

> **Proverbs 27:2** – "*Let another praise you, and not your own mouth; someone else, and not your own lips.*"

Be self assured, but don't consider yourself better than the next person as it unveils a lack of confidence.

On the other hand, sometimes we look at others because we admire something about them. When you see someone who has a gift or an ability that you wish you had, don't look at that person with envy because he or she makes you feel bad about yourself, let him inspire you.

> **Proverbs 14:30** – *"A heart at peace gives life to the body, but envy rots the bones."*

If you find someone attractive, whether man or woman, let that motivate you. For example, if the person looks fit, remember to go to the gym. If his skin glows, it should remind you to eat healthy, exfoliate, and wear plenty of sunscreen. If you admire her silky hair, deep condition yours, and tomorrow, thank that person for your shiny strands.

Suppose you meet someone of wealth. In that event put your nose to the grindstone, and hope in God who will provide for you the means of your enjoyment.

If someone is happy, don't be resentful because you're a miserable pessimist. Let his joy flow through you and bring a smile to your heart. Your feelings and thoughts show through your expressions. If you're walking around with animosity and bitterness, that's what your character will exude—and that is not attractive. Should you meet a happy couple, don't be jealous because you are living life alone; be glad and praise God for the works He has in store for you and your awaited soul mate. Remember, genuine beauty comes from within: if you are feeding yourself positive statements throughout your life while seeking God, that particular magnetism will radiate through you like a glistening star.

It's up to each of us to make the best of what we are. Have you ever noticed a secure, overweight person with a fun, vivacious attitude? You are pleasingly drawn to them, aren't you? You too can accept your present circumstances and spread good cheer while making any favorable adjustments in personal appearance or attitude. So go...walk with a glad spirit and pour forth sweetness and light. :o)

> **Proverbs 17:22** – *"A cheerful heart is good medicine, but a crushed spirit dries up the bones."*

Now suppose you are the target. Have you ever been hurt by someone's remarks or comments toward you? And the nicer your tone the more impolite that person comes across? That is a very unconfident individual using your kindness as a leeway to feel better about him or herself in a warped kind of way. In a situation like this one, you have to remember his rudeness to you is self-conflicted weeping; so hold your head high and pray for your antagonist as you walk away. By doing so you are satisfying God. Love mankind, but don't look for others' approval.

Civilization is fixated on visual appearance to such extent that some people go around thinking everybody is supposed to look and dress according to their viewpoints. In actuality, their points of view are trivial and ridiculous. A group of individuals just like you and I decide what hair, fashion and other trends are set at any given time. That doesn't mean you have to agree with their decision making. If you like to dress faddish, then great. But if you do, that doesn't give you the right to be critical of those who don't. Scripture mentions nothing about vogue or trends, so whose say-so is it anyway?

And when you reach a certain age, there's no need to stamp an "I'm old" seal on yourself by dressing the way others want to see you. The idea that people within a certain age group "shouldn't wear this" or "must wear that" is just another set of rules made up and adhered to by a group of followers.

Once you realize it doesn't matter what people think, you can stop beating yourself up unnecessarily. Relax and be you. All our bodies will return to powdered dust someday. Cover thyself in whatever makes you feel good until your cookie crumbles. And put your energy toward the ideal soul in which you shall live forever. Never consider yourself old, just be thankful for every year added to your blessed long life, as not everyone is that fortunate.

> **1 Timothy 2:9-10** *(New King James version)* – *"In like manner also, that women adorn themselves in modest apparel, with propriety and moderation, not with braided hair or gold or pearls or costly clothing, but, which is proper for women professing godliness, with good works."*

These verses need to be understood in the context of when Paul wrote them: this description of spiffy hair, jewels and fancy clothes refers to the ordinary beautification used in prostitution back then. So a modern comparison needs to be considered. Clothing was a practical necessity during that time, yet today it is often more a style and fashion statement.

> **Romans 12:2** – *"Do not conform any longer to the pattern of this world, but be transformed by the renewing of your mind. Then you will be able to test and approve what God's will is—His good, pleasing and perfect will."*

Only you can uncover your secret self (a very important component to one's character). Build your spirit—and what I mean by that is, allow God to chisel you as an individual from the inside out—and your soul will be fulfilled. But first you have to stop looking for flaws you see in others and focus on the ones that belong to you. For example, find your identity, make up your own mind, decide for yourself what you will wear, and don't judge another for how they are clothed. Worry not what people say or think, only hope that God sees you as good and righteous, as it is His heart you should gladden.

Delve into news to find out facts yourself so that you may reach a decision without walking blindfolded with another blind man. And if you are ever unsure about what you should or should not do, don't ask another thinker at a loss, ask God. He has all the answers, and will eventually bring any uncertainty to light if that is His will. His responses will be given to you at His time, not yours; so don't sit around watching the clock. Just continue your walk in faith.

It is God's job to judge, not ours.

> **Matthew 7:1** – "*Judge not, that you be not judged*" (New King James Version).

Galatians 5:14-15 – Live by the Spirit: "*Love your neighbor as yourself. If you keep on biting and devouring each other, watch out or you will be destroyed by each other.*"

If you find yourself picking someone apart, knock those bitter thoughts right out of your head! Replace them with kind gestures. Find something nice to say about that person. If you look deep enough into his (or her) eyes, which lead to his heart, you will find beauty. It may be smothered by hurt, guilt, low self-esteem and no telling what else, but he is still a child of God. Should he reap evil, then pray for him from a distance. Fill your mind with love, not hate. Find God in everyone you meet. A kind word to another could change his or her life forever.

Proverbs 16:24 – "*Pleasant words are a honeycomb, sweet to the soul and healing to the bones.*"

When you help others make positive changes in their lives, it always makes for a blissful celebration!

Give, give and give abundantly. Give with a hug; give with a smile; give with a compliment or a helping hand. Give your wages, your time, your ears, your heart, your prayers and your hope. Stop judging and start giving.

Proverbs 19:17 – *"He who is kind to the poor lends to the Lord, and He will reward him for what he has done."*

13

UNMASK

Tackle Your Addiction

Only those who are faced with this puzzling malady of drug and alcohol addiction can fully understand the strong desire that goes along with this complex tendency. The person with the compulsion sees the problem but fails to take hold of it. It's much like seeing your self trapped in a fishbowl with what seems like no way out. Have you ever been there? I have.

Again, you are being fooled by your attacker. He has you trapped in another complicated entanglement, one that is sugarcoated with the idea of an escape to a secret hideaway place that will leave you to forget about all of your troubles for a while. It's his surefire way of making you find pleasure in the predicament while gradually sucking you under the killer wave as humiliation repeats itself.

I was strangled by the notion that because of my sensitivity to OTC (over the counter) medicine, alcohol was the only thing I could lean on to assist with any phobias (anxiety, insomnia, etc.) I encountered. This was good in the sense that I never became dependent on prescription or street drugs, but bad in that the reliable firewater only added fuel to my flame. Genetic likelihood, emotional stress and social atmosphere were all contributing factors. And more impulsive than compulsive, my behavior was highly sporadic in that I was an occasional tippler. Never drinking during the day or on a regular basis, I consumed alcohol only during social gatherings or if stressed out at night. This gave me all the more reason to refuse to believe that I belonged in the problem drinker's category.

But alcohol began to take me places my heart wasn't willing to go. And the on again-off again erratic aftereffects eventually amplified to a worrisome peak, which left me forced to act on necessary changes.

> **Ephesians 5:18** – *"Do not get drunk on wine, which leads to debauchery. Instead, be filled with the spirit."*

This is not to say you shouldn't drink alcohol. Alcohol itself is not impure by sin, but it is the addiction and drunkenness you must refrain from.

Ecclesiastes 9:7 – *"Go, eat your food with gladness, and drink your wine with a joyful heart, for it is now that God favors what you do."*

John 2:1-11 talks about how Jesus changed water into wine. That amazing stunner, which occurred in Cana of Galilee, was *"the first of His miraculous signs"* through which *"He thus revealed His glory, and His disciples put their faith in Him."*

Although the cause of this so-called disease has not yet been established, apparently chemical imbalances in the brain cause impulsive behavior and intense desire. This disadvantage can be regulated using a careful and methodical approach. The severity of this confusing mind boggler varies from person to person. And from what I gather, dependency on any other drug has the same effect: those with an addictive personality have their doors wide open.

If this topic does pertain to you, take heed in this serious matter considering your vulnerability so that you are not defenseless like a sitting duck waiting for assault. You have to be the one to close the passageway and fasten it shut, or your predicament will grow as big as the moon and leave you as little as nothing. It's a fight within, and you have to dig deep to get to the root of it.

Wallowing in self-appeasement leads to immoral contemplation and will eventually flurry into disgrace and shame. Most of my humbling experiences were brought about by nothing more than oblivious intoxication—times I can never change or make different. So I continue to push forward toward complete entirety until I can rest assured that I am the best that I can be. Many of you facing the same challenge may not realize that the fears (anxiety, insomnia, obsessive thinking, etc.) that come with this complex disorder have proliferated from the substance itself. If you can get a grip long enough to get the poison out of your system, you will see significant improvement both mentally and physically. And concerns of the mind you once fled from will begin to dissipate, leaving you more in control of your thoughts and actions, consequently curtailing your desire to use.

If you have the slightest concerns of addiction, you are most likely a good candidate for immediate attention. For starters, back off of the substance completely, or it will grow like a deadly fungus. During that time you have to acknowledge the critical situation and decide through prayer, a course of action for your individual needs. And if you can't seem to stop on your own, help is always just a phone call away. You will find a reference in the back of this book. Keep in mind: the longer you wait the harder it will be to tackle. You have to want to change. And I declare with God all things are possible.

Ask God to take away those urges and show you the way to recovery. Be determined and keep the faith. Wait patiently and think positively about the outcome, but never let the austerity of this affliction slip your mind. And thank your Savior as if your prayers have already been answered.

> **Psalm 42:5** – *"Why are you downcast, O my soul? Why so disturbed within me? Put your hope in God, for I will yet praise Him, my savior and my God."*

Let Him be your Authority and He will send you angels. God always appoints me messengers in times of need. And between those heavenly couriers and my true friends, I consider them all angels on earth.

From experience, I know He will pull you out of your pickle if you simply trust. For many years, I tried several ways to fix my problem on my own, and always ended up back at first base sunk deeper than before. Once you give Him the go ahead, the time it takes for God to lift you up is short compared to the endless time it takes otherwise. Don't waste another moment in sinking sand—climb on His rock. And whatever route your Advisor chooses for you, take this along: Reveal your true self as you are taken by surprise—the most beautiful and unique colors made especially for you. Like a stone from the earth's surface, you were exclusively made. You are your one and only, so treat yourself with tender love and care. And begin your new walk in the fruit of the Spirit:

> **Galatians 5:22-23** – *"But the fruit of the spirit is love, joy, peace, patience, kindness, goodness, faithfulness, gentleness and self control."*

ANGELS ON EARTH

14

CLEAN AND FIT

Cleanse Your Mind and Body

1 Corinthians 10:31 – "*So whether you eat or drink or whatever you do, do it all for the glory of God.*"

Stomaching greasy burgers and sitting around like a clay pot are not examples of glorification to our Higher Power! Overindulgence of any kind will bring ruin to the human body.

Look at your reflection in the mirror and observe from head to toe at every angle. You will see an original model structured by the hand of a Genius—and a by-product of your daily habits and lifestyle. If you're motivated it will show, and if you're a slacker, slouch will be displayed.

It takes performance to achieve good things in life, including the promise of the Spirit. We all know that adequate sleep, clean environment, healthy eating habits and exercise, along with beating stress by a positive outlook, stave away plumpness and impurities—hence reducing depression and illnesses. Such acts also exhibit utmost respect for one's self and Supreme Being.

Yet a considerable amount of the general public lies around procrastinating while awaiting their pizza delivery—after complaining all day about the way they look and feel! Although it seems that if you have been idle for a while your energy would skyrocket, this is not the case. Lethargy is a sedentary side effect. Exercise deficit, poor eating habits and mental pressure all cause exhaustion, lack of motivation and debilitating—and sometimes fatal—ailments.

Well aware of the repercussions, a vast majority of the population continues to live life unbothered by the notion that their neglectful behavior will eventually catch up, leaving them miserable and discouraged. It's as if they are oblivious to such worldwide knowledge and understanding. When left entangled in a web woven in repeated doctor's visits, prescription medications and mental despair, they're somehow convinced that they are the unfortunate ones who have been hit with a stroke of bad luck!

> **1 Corinthians 6:19-20** – *"Do you not know that your body is a temple of the Holy Spirit, who is in you, whom you have received from God? You are not your own; you were bought at a price. Therefore honor God with your body."*

If drive is not already deep-seated in you, acquiring it will be a challenge, but your motivation level *can* be elevated. It will require great effort to a certain point, but once you meet that mark, it's a breeze from there. Watching your body transform to your liking, and having a clear mind and oodles of energy to partake in fun sports and activities, will make it easy for you to want to stay on the health-kick track. If you are used to sitting around on your tail, eating processed foods and thinking negatively, then that's what your booty will order. But if you are well-nourished in mind, body and spirit, health-giving is what it craves. No matter how much discipline you have, temptation is right around the corner. And when you are enticed, your determination decides which is more appealing: a healthy way of life that enables you to get the best out of your journey or dragging around a feeble bag of bones while awaiting earthly departure.

When allured by the ruler of darkness, you must slap him back to hell by crushing instant gratification with a rational train of thought. Whatever cognitive reasoning works for you use it! Whether it's a vision of you at your maximum climbing Mount Everest or a picture of yourself overcoming an ongoing hardship in life while physically and mentally on top of the world, you can do it! Remember *willpower*—both "will" and "power"—stems from the mind.

God's hand is always stretched out to you, but you have to reach for Him in order to make that connection. This hookup will get you through any barrier in life. If you've had difficulty outshining transgression in the past, try doing it for God—after all, look what He has done for you. He constantly sends blessings our way, shouldn't we respond by showing our appreciation? Think of Him when you are tested and that should help you call the turn.

Do you feel you've been gypped of good wishes? Don't give up hope as God is waiting to lay His hands on you. Remember, as long as you reflect in prayer and pray in faith you will be acknowledged.

> **Matthew 7:7** – "*Ask and it will be given to you; seek and you will find; knock and the door will be opened to you.*"

He may take you a different route than you had hoped for, but His counter will be advantageous to you in the long run. Put your trust in God!

> **Psalm 91:1-4** – *"He who dwells in the shelter of the Most High will rest in the shadow of the Almighty. I will say of the Lord, 'He is my refuge and my fortress, my God, in whom I trust.' Surely He will save you from the fowler's snare and from the deadly pestilence. He will cover you with His feathers, and under His wings you will find refuge; His faithfulness will be your shield and rampart."*

Proper diet and exercise will also improve your mental stability. Maintaining ideal weight by exerting more energy than you consume is key.

Portion-controlled daily consumption of whole grains, fruits, vegetables and lean proteins, rightly balanced five times a day, is my menu of choice. Breakfast, lunch and dinner, with a snack in between, are beneficial. Eating every three to four hours along with my workout regimen helps keep me charged. Then I reward myself with a sweet treat on Sunday or maybe something fried every few months—if I give in. A splurge now and then helps keep me in that perpetual healthful groove 95 percent of the time. So, for the most part I eat for sustenance, not pleasure. "Bunches" and I also enjoy juicing with fresh fruits, veggies and wheatgrass on a daily basis. It's very time-consuming, but well worth it as it gives us a lot of energy and helps us to glow.

You will find my personal cuisine routine and systematized workout schedule on my website, along with spiritually driven motivational tips and an exercise program designed especially for you. I have been accredited as a certified personal trainer by the American Council on Exercise since 2002.

Take God's hand...let's get started!

15

PAINT ME PINK!

Be Simply Happy

Outline me happy, shade me glad, color me the best day I can possibly have!

Latch onto good cheer and put on a happy face! Don't take for granted the many gifts that surround you. If you have a case of the blahs then you are most likely the one who brought the glumness to your life. You can't find happiness only when things are going your way. You have to make every day unforgettable in this ever-so-changeable world.

My sister Linda often says to me, "Make the very best out of every minute because after that moment is gone, you can only reflect." And she lives those words to the fullest. Being the most positive person I know, she takes advantage of God's creation by gardening and taking photographs of all kinds of creatures that visit her lively backyard—from hummingbirds to bees that gather around her many flowers. Her love is painting and her artwork is usually of nature and animals. While brushing and daubing she recites scripture as if she wrote the books herself. You can see selections of her glorified work at the end of this chapter and on my website listed in the back of this book.

It's the simple things money can't buy that make for fond recollections. In elementary school, saluting The Pledge and singing "My Country Tis' of Thee" before the day began are warm reflections of mine. "Protect us by Thy Might, Great God our King"—how proud I felt as an American and a child of God. Or when the scent of rain meant it was safe to splash in puddles, bringing mud-squished feet and a stumped big toe. I think back to the joyful voices shouting "Wait for me!" as they rushed to the musical truck—and can still taste the bubblegum found in my cone-shaped ice cream when I licked my way to the bottom. Did you ever thumb through the green, green grass in hopes for a four leaf clover? "Wholesome gladness" is how I describe these kinds of memories.

Our simplistic nature as children shouldn't end with adolescence; in fact, this kind of heart helps preserve our youth. What makes you feel good that money can't buy? I love to hang my cotton and linen garments in the sunshine to dry for a stark white result and air fresh smell. Or gaze at the detail in flowers in amazement at their beauty. I try to keep fresh petals around if possible because they make me feel good. It doesn't have to be a bushel; just one little daisy will do. My daughter's favorite is the water lily. When blooms begin to wilt, I break them off at the top of the stem and let them float in water in a clear glass bowl along with a few leaves—the effect is much like a lily and it always reminds me of her.

Vintage cars and trucks are another love of mine, so I'm planning a photo shoot by a few old classics to have for my portfolio. Every day do something different than yesterday, and make it a tad bit sweeter. Whatever tickles your fancy, all you have to do is act on it. And while you're at it, don't forget to laugh!

So, when snowflakes fall, don't complain of the wintry brisk and nothing much to do; grab your thermals and get cozy by a fire. There are so many invigorating activities to choose from when it flurries: from sipping hot cocoa to a snowball fight or sledding down a hill. And when nighttime falls and God has taken away all the fluffy clouds, go outside and try to count the stars in the crystal clear sky. Good luck!

Make all seasons worthy of fun. In the springtime everything comes to life, so awaken your mind with lively intentions. Let new ideas come to thought as change is often good. Lack of action will cause your vitality to fester. And the spring time of the year is great for recharging, so be creative when planning anything from a fun outfit to a cookout with friends.

When the leaves fall, energize yourself with a hike in a safe and beautiful place. Breathe in cool fresh air while admiring the scenery of God's well-timed changes. The winter, when the holidays roll around is my all-time favorite experience of the year; sharing, giving and singing aloud, feasting and communing. It's a time to share our many blessings while we celebrate the birth of Jesus Christ our Lord and Savior. Although, for Him, everyday should be a day of celebration!

You, my friend, are duty-bound for enchantment in your life! Make it good for yourself. As the saying goes, "progress gives purpose" so reach for the sky as that is your limit. Choose any color from the rainbow—or how about more than just one tone? After all, that vibrant prism was made for you and me as a reminder of Him.

> **Genesis 9:12-16** – *"And God said, '...I have set My rainbow in the clouds, and it will be a sign of the*

covenant between Me and the earth. Whenever I bring clouds over the earth and the rainbow appears in the clouds, I will remember My covenant between Me and you and all living creatures of every kind. Never again will the waters become a flood to destroy all life. Whenever the rainbow appears in the clouds, I will see it and remember the everlasting covenant between God and all living creatures of every kind on the earth.'"

Linda Ferguson

CROCODILE
DOCK

MY FIRST CLASSIC CAR SHOOT

16

GLORY TO GOD!

Kudos to Our Most High God

As the sun lights up the daytime and the moon gives luminescence, the waters teem with living beings and the seeds bear plants, the eagles soar across the sky and the lionesses hunt in packs, we forget...

> **Genesis 1:26-27** – *"Then God said, 'Let Us make man in Our image, in Our likeness, and let him rule over the fish of the sea and the birds of the air, over the livestock, over all the earth, and over all the creatures that move along the ground.' So God created man in His own image, in the image of God He created him; male and female He created them."*

How can one say there is no God? With such ingenious, well-planned and calculated craftiness, what are the chances of evolution occurring simply because the world turns? Think about the countless distinctive creatures of all shapes and colors, alive and extraordinarily nurtured. The bees feed from the flowers and the flowers from rain. Ponder God's reckoning when He perfectly marked the days and the seasons and the years. Believe in miracles—they surround you every day.

When we are born into this thing called life, it's as if we jump on a train that has traveled for years, but we have no clue where it's been or where it's taking us. We just start living according to our environments and what's going on around us—things we see, what we hear, touch and feel. We milk life for what we perceive as worth: material possessions, fortune and fame. Yet we pass right by the most essential elements that surround us, the ones that make a difference during and after we have completed our short-lived time here on earth.

> **Genesis 1:1** – *"In the beginning God created the heavens and the earth."*

You really don't think God went above and beyond to create this heavenly structure so that we never acknowledge His works, do you? So that we idolize man and not Him, praise superstars and forget His worth? If fans could devote a fraction of the time worshiping their Lord and Savior that they spend on their worldly heroes, their time would be well spent. Sure, we should appreciate talent and be inspired by those with dedication and drive, and I am not implying otherwise. The point being, let your expressions show God's works in you while you see His love in others. Because He is the One who lives in us and we are those who beam His light. So, it is God whom we should idolize.

While writing this inspirational, I lost my very special twin brother to a sudden passing on October 29, 2009, as his heart gave out on him. As mentioned in the beginning of this book, we are the youngest of seven. So his death was certainly a shock to me, as well as to everyone who knew him. My mother was crushed. But she keeps herself occupied with work, friends and church as the power of God enriches her life with a greater understanding of His purpose.

I remember Jack as he was—a very loving, giving, funny, good-looking and smart young man. He knew Christ, and because he believed, I trust his spirit and soul will live forever.

Until Jack's passing I had never lost someone with whom I had such a bond, so reality really jolted me! Unfortunately in life, we must bear the brunt of such tragedies whether past, present or future. It is inevitable we will all face the end of this life just as my brother has. So what makes the most sense is to forget about the worldly things here on earth and focus more on glorification of our God in the Most High. He is the One who has control over all of His handiwork, which includes the believing soul—the essence of personhood that is promised eternal life.

Praise God!

IN MEMORY OF JACK

Precious soul, I'll think of you each and every day.
The handwritten scripture you left behind lets me know that you're OK.
The love you shared while you were here has touched many hearts,
Growing among the children you shared such a part.
It will spread through generations to come, as you meant it to,
All because of you, Jack, all because of you.
We shared a stroller, baby bed and a tree-hut too;
You told me I was beautiful, unlike most brothers do. :o)
We built sandcastles, fed seagulls and caught tadpoles at the creek;
You shot my butt with a BB gun—claimed you were aiming at my feet.
I watched your school plays, and proudly so,
"Eat your heart out, Fonzie!" as you stole the show.
I cheered you on at your games, football and baseball; became your team queen.
Rest in peace as you are set free
And I'll see you in Heaven when it's time for me…

I LOVE YOU JACK!

MY BROTHER JACK

INDIANS
12 121

ALL OF US

MOM & DAD

IN A NUTSHELL

(My Conclusion)

Like Gump's box of chocolates, life's adventures come in a variety of assortments—and "you never know what you're gonna get!"

We all face hardships in life. This book is meant to help you become more watchful and aware of temptation while exercising acts of love instead of hostility. Doing so will enable you to face challenges with less difficulty and sometimes stop them before they come about.

Do away with the lies and impurities that have been invading your mind, body, and soul for as long as you can remember—deceptions you thought you had no control over, but have come to realize you do. Become tuned in to the fact that you are now head honcho and child of the Most High God and nothing will stand in your way!

> **Proverbs 3:5-8** – "*Trust in the Lord with all your heart and lean not on your own understanding; in all your ways acknowledge Him, and He will make your paths straight. Do not be wise in your own eyes; fear the Lord and shun evil. This will bring health to your body and nourishment to your bones.*"

> **Romans 8:26-28** – "*...the Spirit helps us in our weakness. We do not know what we ought to pray for, but the Spirit Himself intercedes for us with groans that words cannot express. And He who searches our hearts knows the mind of the Spirit, because the Spirit intercedes for the saints in accordance with God's will. And we know that in all things God works for the good of those who love Him, who have been called according to His purpose.*"

Many are cynical and stay shy of theology because it seems so fictitious. For example, even though it's mentioned several times in the Bible, there's a lot of controversy about the motto "Jesus is coming soon." Because to most ears that means in a lickety-split, and we've been hearing that for decades. I believe Jesus will definitely be back. But as the Bible mentions in **Matthew 24:36-42**, no one knows when He will return except for His Father, not even the angels of Heaven. So "expect it anytime" is how I perceive the message. And remember too:

> **2 Peter 3:8** – "*But do not forget this one thing, dear friends: With the Lord a day is like a thousand years, and a thousand years are like a day.*"

God's mysteries without a doubt go beyond our wildest dreams. But to have faith means you have to believe what you don't understand or what may seem impossible. If we weren't born into this wondrous life it would also be hard to imagine, wouldn't it?

> **Mark 5:34** – "*And* [Jesus] *said to her, 'Daughter, your faith has healed you. Go in peace and be freed from your suffering.'*"

So go with good intentions. Trust and be set free.

> **Philippians 4:13 – "I can do all things through Christ who gives me strength"** (New King James Version).

A PLACE IN MY HEART

My thanks to:

God, for using me to write this book, together with Your many blessings!

I LOVE YOU!!!

My husband, John Paul Somers, for your love, patience, support, and encouragement

My daughter Ashley Abercrombie, for your love, comfort, and assurance

My mother, Beverly Ann Gunn, for instilling so much love in me

My brothers and sisters, (Jack Wright, Terri Kingry, Buddy Wright, Cathy Wright, Diane Rutherford, and Linda Ferguson), for all of your special ways

My mother-in-law, Maryann Petri Somers, for being my "angel on the seventh floor"

Linda and Michael Ferguson, for your prayers, teaching, and ears

Gary and Wendy Anderson, for all of the fun fellowshipping

Cliff, Julie, Will, and Matthew Shirah, for your friendship, and all of your kind words

Susan Landrum, for always being there

Lisa Boecker, for the prayers, many laughs, and giggles! :O)

Luigi Morabito, pour votre devouement en temps de besoin

Author's website information:

www.julieannsomers.com

Addiction Treatment Resource

If you or someone you love is struggling with drug or alcohol addiction or a related behavioral health issue, help is available. CRC Health Group offers a comprehensive, nationwide network of personalized treatment services including detoxification, outpatient, inpatient, and residential treatment. For over three decades, CRC programs have helped individuals and families reclaim and enrich their lives. For more information, visit www.crchealth.com or call (877) 637-6237.